Dealing

With

Bloodline Patterns

How To Overcome Negative Family Patterns

Copyright © 2019

By
Chris Emeruo

No part of this publication may be reproduced, stored in retrieval system, or be transmitted in any form or by any means, mechanical, electronic or otherwise (except for brief quotations in printed view) without prior consent of the author or publisher.

ISBN 978-978-958-240-2

Bible quotations are taken from:
King James Version (KJV) except otherwise indicated.

RIVERSIDE PUBLICATIONS

P.O. Box 13159 IKEJA, LAGOS.

Telephone: +234-8124429859.

www.chrisemeruo.org

info@chrisemeruo.org.

Acknowledgement

In the course of writing this book, I was blessed to receive immense help and support from many gifted hands and associates. I owe them profound appreciation.

The first person to thank is Tony Nze, who painstakingly edited the manuscript of this book. May God enrich him with more grace and wisdom to enable him fulfill his divine assignment on humanity.

I would also like to express my special thanks of gratitude to Danny Barnabas, Anne Obiajunwa, Innocent Emeruo, Andy Momalife, Cedric Okonji and Deaconess Yemi Ogbe for their invaluable contributions to the publication of this masterpiece. May God enrich them with Immeasurable blessings.

Contents

Acknowledgement

Introduction

Introduction

The term "Family Patterns" or "Bloodline Patterns" are very common slangs among religious folks these days. Literally speaking, or in general sense, bloodline patterns show how happenstances repeat themselves in a family lineage. If any incident repeats itself regularly in a family, say yearly, biyearly, in the space of 5, 10 or 15 years, we say a "Bloodline Pattern" exists as far as such incident is concerned.

A bloodline pattern could be "Positive or Negative" in nature. We term it "Positive Patterns" if the reoccurring incidents are good, pleasant, progressive and of course desirable by members of that family. But when the reoccurring incidents are bad, unpleasant, detestable, saddening and of course undesirable, they are branded "Negative Patterns".

Every man on earth earnestly desires and prays that only good things should happen to him and his lineage. It is rare and abnormal to see anyone rejoicing when bad things happen to his family, especially on a regular basis. Succinctly put, almost everyone frowns at the incessant reoccurrences of bad things in his family. In fact, in many societies and cultures, families are viewed to be under a curse if their lives are associated with too many bad and unexplainable narratives.

If your family is enjoying a positive pattern of events, such that favour and gladness have become your lot, I congratulate you. But if bad, painful and unpleasant experiences are your lot, you need serious help, and that's the essence of this book.

Why do you need to deal with bloodline patterns? The answer is simple. Your life will go in the direction of your patterns.

There are some fundamental keys that can help to extricate you from negative bloodline patterns and open to you, doors of abundant blessings. It is these cardinal keys that I have unveiled in the pages of this book. I am strongly persuaded that if you tenaciously adhere to the spirit inspired teachings contained in this book, you will never be held bound by any negative pattern that runs in your bloodline.

You need freedom. You need joy. You need things to work for you. That is why Jesus died for you on the Cross of Calvary. God's full loads of blessing are for us. He has not called us to live a life of 50 percent or even 70 percent, but for us to live a life of 100 percent.

If you are living a life short of what Jesus has paid for – a life below your calling, a life full of failure, hopelessness and sadness in spite of so many resolutions and efforts, a life characterized by shame and disgrace, then you need a touch of God's finger. Solution to such problems do not come by mere wishful thinking, it comes by clear understanding of the root causes of the problems and a conscious step to extricate yourselves via the instrumentality of the word of God and prayers.

This book unveils the diversities and causal factors of negative patterns in many families. It educates us on how to break negative jinxes and enjoy the divine favours and prosperity God intends for us.

With this book in your hands, you are armed to enforce a change in your life and family. You are now on top of your matters and will no longer be tossed around by the waves of happenstances in your family. Your dreams and aspirations will receive wings to fly.

As you peruse the divine truths revealed in this book with unalloyed mind frame, I bid you divine help to assimilate the truth, and the grace to say enough is enough to the negative patterns of events running in your family.

Shalom!

Chris Emeruo (2019)

Chapter 1

Understanding Bloodline Patterns

"Remember the days of old,
consider the years of all generations.
Ask your father, and he will inform you,
your elders, and they will tell you." **(Deut. 32:7)**

In 2012, I ministered to a woman in Lagos, Nigeria. She was in her late thirties, soundly educated and beauty personified. Surprisingly, she was working as a house-help, somewhere in Lagos. At first, I couldn't understand why in the midst of superfluity of opportunities in the city, and her level of education, she elected to do such job our society usually ranks ignoble.

More worrisome was that as at the time we met, she had been on this job for more than five years. She had no plans to quit, no plans to further her education, in fact, no plans to better her life. She was deeply engrossed in the work. I probed deeply to decipher why she was fulfilled being a family house help. I was amazed she could not offer any tangible reason.

In the swing of discussion, I came to discover that her parents were alive, and they were also servants to a family in their village. They were not just the usual house helps we know today. Their case was more acute and pathetic, such that they surrendered themselves to a family. They had lived a great part of their lives in that family. In fact, they gave birth to all their kids there. As at the time we met, her parents were still residing in that family's house.

Further interrogation also revealed that her grandparents had similar history. They lived, worked and served the king of their village for several years.

This lady, unknowingly, aligned herself to the patterns of events and happenstances transpiring in their family for a very long time. This was so, despite the fact that she claimed to be born again and committed to church activities. What a pity that some people still live in the past despite being in the present.

Led by the Holy Spirit, I ministered the word of God to her and taught her key kingdom principles and spiritual weapons that will help to disengage and extricate her from the enslavement and negative patterns of events that run in their family bloodline.

I am excited to inform you that she heeded to my advice and was utterly emancipated from the stronghold of the enemy. All the unpleasant pattern of events she was labouring under for a long time gave way and she started living a happy life.

What Do We Mean By Bloodline Pattern

Bloodline pattern is said to exist in a family if some events or incidents occur repeatedly, regularly, seasonally or occasionally, such that almost every inmate of the family, or anyone who knows the family, knows that there is a high probability of such incidents reoccurring at a particular time, in a particular way, to that particular people.

For an issue to be branded a bloodline pattern, the incidences have to happen to a person or a people repeatedly, regularly, sequentially or intermittently.

So to say, that thing that happens to you repeatedly or intermittently is a pattern,

and if members of your family in the past experienced it, and it still happens to the present generation, and may likely happen to the future generation if not halted, it can be referred to as family or bloodline pattern.

Some family patterns are good, pleasant and desirable. We refer to them as "positive bloodline patterns." For example, there are families where people live to a very long age. Some homes usually produce great brains and the best in schools. Some families are renowned for producing high quality leaders in the society. There are some other families where many people get rich without much effort, etc.

However, some bloodline patterns tend toward the negative. Such patterns are detestable, unpleasant and undesirable. There are deluge of examples of negative bloodline patterns. For want of space, we will discuss few examples in the course of this book. But one thing is sure, negative bloodline patterns are certainly not the will of God for His children.

How Bloodline Patterns Start

Every bloodline pattern; whether positive or negative, originates from a source. It has an origin. It starts from somebody, somewhere or an encounter. It could start from an individual who lived a kind of life, or, who provoked some blessings or curses as the case may be. The effects of such deeds now trickle down, impact and run through the lineage from one generation to another.

The action of the provoker of the bloodline pattern is important in determining whether the pattern will be positive or negative. If the action is good, it will provoke blessings cum positive things in the lineage. But if the actions are evil, negative reactions follow.

The simple message here is that nothing just happens. For every action, there is a reaction; and the reaction depends on what happened in the first instance. This is the secret of the blessings many people are enjoying or the afflictions others are passing through today. Someone called the shot and the game kicked off.

Most times, when we see families that are prosperous, we are tempted to ask, "Why are these people so blessed? Why is it that whatever they touch turns to gold? Why are they so favoured by men? Why do they live so long and healthy?"

The answer is simple. Someone in their lineage became their Abraham that attracted the blessings to his lineage. Similarly, the pains, sufferings and difficulties many people (including some acclaimed Christians in that family) pass through can be painstakingly traced to someone in that lineage who did some evils that attracted negativity.

Unfortunately, most times, they may not even know the reasons or the forces behind what they are passing through in life.

Discover the Prevalent Patterns in Your Lineage

In the course of writing this book, I undertook in-depth studies on individuals, families and communities in regard to bloodline patterns. Some of my findings were amazing and affirm the veracity of the assertion that bloodline patterns actually exist.

Samuel, my close associate, disclosed a pattern that was predominant in his family. According to him, all the men who got married from his family ended up abandoning their wives and children. So to say, women in this family usually raised their children alone. This was a pattern every member of the family was conversant with. It happened without the husband and wife bargaining for it. It was either the man left them and remarried, or he stayed far away, indirectly putting the burden of the family on the wife.

According to the story, usually, the couples do not consciously or wilfully agree to go their separate ways at first. It may begin with a new job which may warrant one of the partners to leave the state or the country. It could just be an ordinary business trip, before you know it, this temporal separation solidifies to permanent and irreversible separation.

The sad thing about all these, is that this family is a renowned Christian family. As at the time of writing this book, Samuel's family is the only family that has not toed this line.

Samuel is not oblivious to the fact that the spirit behind the pattern will really want to show up and battle against his own marriage. So he is not taking chances. He is not giving room for whatever will bring separation between him and his wife. No excuse is genuine enough to permit his family stay aloof of him until he has built the capacity to tackle such a pattern.

Temptation came at a point when his wife got an appointment in Abuja. The pay and other welfare packages attached to the job were huge. Consequently, the woman resolved to accept the job. The implication is that she will relocate to Abuja, leaving the husband behind in Lagos.

To cut the story short, Samuel did not need a seer to tell him that the prevalent pattern is fighting to show up in his family, using the instrumentality of a good job. Divine wisdom prevailed and he stood his ground and insisted that the woman should reject the offer. He won at last.

Apart from this Abuja offer, many other mouth-watering opportunities that come their way are such that if accepted will keep the family apart.

This buttresses the fact that the spirit behind any pattern persists in its battles until those involved yield and the pattern prevails. But those who know their God persist in the battle until victory over the ancient patterns is ascertained and the patterns are broken.

I strongly suggest that you take your time to study and uncover the pattern of events in your family. So done, you will discover the positive packages and strength of your bloodline and maximize them. You will also uncover the negative patterns of events in your bloodline and consciously treat them accordingly.

The Devil Rides on Your Bloodline Pattern to Harm You

The devil is very subtle, cunning and intelligent. To prosecute his devilish enterprises on a man or his family and to thwart people's destiny, sometimes he surreptitiously adopts the pattern of events that transpire in that family. The implication most times is that rather than seeing the devil behind any particular problem, the people presume that it is normal – it is the way it happens with us.

We are used to this. Thus, they do little or nothing about it. So to say, even the devil, our eternal enemy, maximizes the bloodline pattern to prosecute his assignments.

The Devil Can Use Anybody to Enforce a Pattern

I have heard some people say that if you are very careful and play your card well, the devil can never enforce a pattern on you. Anyways, it depends on what they mean by "playing your card well". If you are only talking of using human rationality and strength to defeat the devil's wiles, then I am sorry to inform you that you will be disappointed. It simply won't work. You cannot beat the devil with the armoury of the flesh. Only the power of Jesus can disarm and overcome the devil. Only the blood of the lamb can silence the devil for life. The bible says "And they overcame him by the blood of the Lamb, and by the word of their testimony..." (Rev. 12:11). It didn't say they overcame by their knowledge, wisdom or strength. The strategy has not changed, and the weapon of warfare has not changed too.

A woman was deeply bothered that five of her female children were not getting married, in fact, many female children in that family lineage end up as single mothers.
The woman called her daughters and expressed her bother that they are not getting married, and advised that they should not trivialize any good relationship they find themselves.

The last daughter who felt age was still on her side boasted and told the mother that nothing on earth will make her not to marry. She boasted that whatever is holding others bound in the family and preventing them from getting married cannot prevail over her.
Her "big talk and boasting" gladdened her mother's heart and encouraged the family.

Some months later, a very handsome guy that works with one of the big companies in town fell in love with her. As much as she could, she played her roles well to ensure that the relationship lasted.

Unfortunately, she left God aside. She thought human strength was enough.

Three months to the wedding, the devil decided to show her that human strength and intelligence are not enough to fight spiritual battles. She stopped seeing her menses and confided with a friend that she had missed her period for the past two months. She claimed never to have slept with the guy and so have no reason to suspect pregnancy.

Anyways, the devil was looking for someone to use to execute his enterprise, and lo and behold, he has seen one. This lady who happens to know the fiancé, unfortunately revealed this information to him that his wife-to-be is pregnant, that she has not been seeing her period for the past two months.

Out of rage, and confidence that he wasn't responsible for her pregnancy, called off the wedding without verifying the gossip from his partner.

The news spread like wild fire within the neighbourhood causing the lady's mother to weep bitterly. However, she confronted her daughter of the alleged pregnancy, claiming that she had disappointed the family. The lady was heartbroken and insisted that she was not pregnant. She even demanded that they go for medical test to prove her innocence.

After much persuasions and interventions, the man accepted that they should go for a test, but insisted that it must be done by his personal doctor.

To cut the story short, the pregnancy test was negative. The guy didn't believe it. He demanded that another test be carried out in another hospital. Just like the first one, the second test proved negative too.

Two days after the pregnancy test, the lady saw her menses. Shame could not allow the man go back to the girl. And all efforts by people to reunite them failed. The lady argued that the man didn't trust her, and consequently allowed her pass through such emotional pains and humiliation. He didn't even give her the opportunity to explain herself. She thus decided never to marry the guy.

That lady is still single till today. You can see how the devil used her friend to enforce a pattern that is prevalent in the family.

Don't say nothing will happen. Fight it!

Chapter 2

Why One Man's Actions Can Affect His Bloodline

"The LORD said to Jehu,

"Because you have done well in executing what is right in my

eyes, and have done to the house of Ahab

according to all that was in My heart,

your sons of the fourth generations shall sit on the throne of

Israel."

(2 Kings 10:30)

After one of our seminars at the Lagos State University, in 2017, a young man sent me a mail, narrating an ordeal he passes through periodically and requested that we pray along with him. In his mail, he wrote, "This same problem happened to my grandfather when he was alive. My father suffered it before he died. Now, the same thing is happening to me. Why is it so? Must I die of what killed my father? Why do I have to go the way of my ancestors?" I was so touched when I read this part.

Well, some people may hastily adjudge the problem as hereditary. It is natural to do so. As a matter of fact, that was exactly my first thought when I read his mail.

I engaged him in a confab, and in the swing of discussion, it became clearer to me that their case had nothing to do with hereditary alone. There is a spiritual finger that ought to be cut off in that family.

I also know a family of three brothers, who died in auto accident following the same pattern, the eldest brother got involved in a fatal accident on his way to work. Five years later the next man following him died in an accident, five years after, the next man in line also died in an accident.

How do you explain this? Can you call this hereditary? No!

Why One Man's Action Can Affect His Bloodline

The question is, "Why do people of the same bloodline pass through similar circumstances sometimes? What is the secret of Mr. X, suffering what Mr. Y and Z suffered in the same family and what are the reasons why Mr. A, B and C from the same lineage enjoy similar favour?

From my research, I believe that the reasons for bloodline patterns are as follow:

Families Are Tied Together By the Cord of Blood

Members of the same family are tied together by the cord of blood. In the book of Leviticus 17:10-12, God spoke to Moses and Aaron and commanded them not to eat of any animal's blood because the blood is the life of any living organism.

Blood is thick and has a strong bond that connects families together. It was required in the Old Testament for atonement (not flesh and water but blood). The cord of blood has many implications than what the rational mind can elucidate.

Because they are of the same stock, family members share some common traits, idiosyncrasies and habits. Just as they have many things in common in the physical, and have a share in the family physical inheritance, they also have many things in common in the spiritual and share in the spiritual family inheritance; whether good or bad. Most times, they inherit or enjoy similar blessings, and oftentimes, labour under the same kind of challenges. Because of the cord of blood, certain things happen to them regularly or occasionally, which do not necessarily happen to people of other families. That is why we term it "Bloodline Pattern".

Family Traits Can Be Transferred To the Next Generations

Universally, it is a known fact backed with evidence that one generation has some level of influence on another. Family traits are often passed down from parents to children, and this cycle continues for thousands of years except it is intercepted along the line. So, it can be said that one of the major reasons why bloodline patterns are possible is because family traits are transferable from one generation to the subsequent ones.

Some of the traits passed down from one generation to another may be positive and beneficial. However, negative traits are also passed down within the family line.

Organisms Reproduce Their Kind

Each human family has its own culture, unique strength and identifiable weaknesses. Some of these may be the result of genetic inheritance. For example, some families have a history of significant musical, academic or athletic accomplishments passed down from parents to children, to grandchildren and sometimes to great-grandchildren. A lion will beget a lion and a sheep will always beget a sheep.

So, hereditary is one of the major reason why people of the same family look or behave alike in many circumstances.

Certain sicknesses that prevail in a family for many generations may be caused by genetics. People who share the same genetic identity may be predisposed to the same kind of sickness. So, it is possible to see people of the same bloodline experiencing similar sicknesses such as eye problem, diabetes, cancer, among other diseases.

Apart from genetic make-ups that are transferred from one generation to another, other strengths and weaknesses within an individual family culture are the result of its environment or choices. This includes values, priorities and decision-making skills. When negative choices and a bad home environment become deeply entrenched within a family culture, individual members can become self-destructive and unknowingly pass on these traits.

Some of us come from family backgrounds of defeatism, divorce, pessimism, selfishness, greed, anger, addictions and laziness. All these negative traits and habits can be learned and passed on to our children.

The fact is that once a dysfunctional personal behaviour becomes a model or an example to the next generation, the cycle can be repeated over and over again.

In recap, families tend to reproduce their own culture and dysfunctions for generations. For instance, selfish parents often produce selfish children, alcoholic parents are more likely to produce alcoholic children, spousal abusers often produce children who grow up and abuse their spouses, and parents with negative lifestyles and attitudes tend to reproduce offspring who are unproductive and discouraged.

Often, this cycle continues until someone who has seen the light wakes up to say, "Enough is enough". I cannot be part of this anymore. My case should be different.

Chapter 3

Evidence Of Bloodline Patterns In The Bible

"And through your descendants
all the nations of the earth will be blessed
all because you have obeyed me." **(Gen 22:8 NLT)**

Is it in the bible? Are there proofs both in the Old and New Testaments that bloodline patterns exist? Are there scriptures to back such controversial teaching? I guess these and many other similar questions will be running through many rational minds in the Church.

Anyways, since the bible is the final authority of our faith, there is nothing wrong in knowing whether such teaching aligns with the word of God. A painstaking study of some families and generations in the holy book will reveal that there were some persistent, prevalent and unique patterns that were associated with such families or generations. The examples are numerous, but Abraham's lineage will be used as a typical example to drive home our message.

The Study of Abraham's Bloodline

Abraham was the father of Isaac, and Isaac was the father of Jacob. A painstaking study of the bible will show that there were so many positive bloodline patterns associated with Abraham's lineage. Likewise, there were some predominant negative patterns associated with them. Let's see some of the patterns.

Pattern #1
Abraham's Lineage was Associated with Barrenness

One prominent negative pattern Abraham's lineage was associated with is barrenness. A careful study of the scripture shows that Abraham, Isaac and Jacob's wives were all barren for a long period of time before God miraculously intervened and changed their situations.

Abraham's Case

Recall that God promised Abraham that he will father descendants who would out-number the stars in the sky

(Gen.15:5), But this didn't come so easily. Though Sarai his wife eventually became pregnant and bore a child in her old age, she was barren for 25 years. See what the bible says about Sarai:

"But Sarai was barren; she had no child."
(Gen 11:30)

The situation became frustrating to the point that Sarah had to persuade her husband to have a baby with her maid, Hagar.

Isaac's Case

Isaac's wife, Rebecca faced a similar trial just like Abraham's wife. She did not conceive for the first 20 years of her marriage to Isaac. See what the bible says

"And Isaac entreated the LORD for his wife, because she was barren: and the
LORD was entreated of him, and Rebekah his wife conceived."
(Genesis 25:21)
Though Rebecca later conceived and bore twins; Jacob and Esau, who became patriarchs of the Jewish and Edomite nations respectively, the fact remains that Rebecca was barren for 20 years before giving birth.

Jacob's Case

The case of Jacob's wife was not different. Rachel was also barren for 14 years. The bible recorded thus:

"And when Rachel saw that she bare Jacob no children, Rachel envied her sister; and said unto Jacob, Give me children, or else I die.

And Jacob's anger was kindled against Rachel: and he said, am I in God's stead, who hath withheld from thee the fruit of the womb?"

(Gen 30:1-2)

Rachel was the most favourite wife of Jacob. She was also the younger sister of Leah. In line with what happens in Abraham's lineage, she was barren, thus, could not give Jacob children. But thank God it all became history after God opened up her womb and she bore Jacob two sons; Joseph and Benjamin.

Another of Jacob's Wife called Leah was also barren for some years.

"And when the LORD saw that Leah was hated, He opened her womb: but Rachel was barren."

(Gen 29:31)

The bible says the Lord opened Leah's womb. This presupposes that her womb was closed for reasons the bible did not explain. But I believe it was not by coincidence. The same web that entangled other women in the past entangled her also. I strongly believe it's a bloodline pattern that was operating in that family.

Pattern #2
The First Male Children Miss Their Inheritance

Another prevalent negative pattern in Abraham's bloodline was that all their first-borns missed their inheritance as first sons. See examples below:

- Abraham's first born according to the flesh (Ishmael) did not receive the first born inheritance, rather Isaac the second received the blessing.

- Isaac's first born (Esau) didn't get the firstborn inheritance rather Jacob the second son did.

- Jacob's first born (Reuben) did not get the first born inheritance rather Judah did.

- Joseph's first born (Manasseh) did not receive the first born inheritance rather Ephraim the second son did.

- David's first born did not receive the first born inheritance, rather Solomon did. All these were not by coincidence. It was a bloodline pattern that was at work.

Pattern #3

They Were Renown for Telling Lies

Telling lies was another characteristic people in Abraham's lineage were renowned for. As a friend usually puts it, "They had first class degree in telling lies."

Every bible scholar knows that in Genesis chapter 20:2, Abraham lied to Abimelech, the king of Gerrar, about his wife Sarah. For fear of being killed, he lied that Sarah was his sister.

Abraham's son Isaac, also followed the trend. To avert being killed in a foreign land, he lied that his wife was his sister.

"And Isaac dwelt in Gerrar. And the men of the place asked him of his wife; and he said; she is my sister: for he feared to say, she is my wife; lest, said he,
the men of the place should kill me for Rebekah; because she was fair to look upon".

(Gen 26:6-7)

This lying lifestyle continued in his lineage. Many years after, Jacob; Abraham's grandson lied to his father Isaac that he was Esau, just to claim the birthright of the first son (Gen27:19).

Jacob's children toed the line of their family lifestyle. They sold their brother Joseph to the Egyptians and lied to their father that he was devoured by wild beast (Gen 37:29-35).

If you read through the pages of the bible, you will see that the lying pattern continued in that lineage.

Pattern #4
Their Love For Beautiful Women

One prominent trait in Abraham's lineage is that they had proclivity and penchant for fair (beautiful) women.
Abraham married a beautiful wife. See what the bible says:

"As he was about to enter Egypt, he said to his wife Sarai,
"I know what a beautiful woman you are.
When the Egyptians see you, they will say, 'This is his wife.'
Then they will kill me but will let you live.
Say you are my sister, so that I will be treated well for your sake
and my life will be spared because of you."
(Gen. 12:11-13 NIV)

To show that the love for beautiful (fair) women runs in their lineage, Isaac; Abraham's son married a very beautiful wife just like his father did - Like father, like son.

> "So Isaac dwelt in Gerar.
> And the men of the place asked about his wife.
> And he said, "She is my sister";
> for he was afraid to say, "she is my wife,"
> because he thought, "lest the men of the place kill me for
> Rebekah, because she is beautiful to behold".
> **(Gen. 26:6-7 NKJ)**

The flair and proclivity to marry beautiful women did not end with Isaac; it still went down to his son Jacob. In fact, Jacob's case was even worse. He even had to serve his master for another 7 years after serving for the first 7 years, just to marry a particular pretty woman.

> "Now Laban had two daughters; the name of the older was
> Leah, and the name of the younger was Rachel.
> Leah had weak eyes, but Rachel had a lovely figure and was
> beautiful. Jacob was in love with Rachel and said,
> "I'll work for you seven years in return for your younger
> daughter Rachel." Laban said,
> " It's better that I give her to you than to some other man. Stay
> here with me."
> So Jacob served seven years to get Rachel, but they seemed like
> only a few days to him because of his love for her"
> **(Gen 29:16-19 NIV).**

According to the passage above, Jacob preferred Rachel to Leah because she was beautiful in appearance.

Leban deceived Jacob and gave him Leah at night. Jacob discovered this in the morning and demanded to know why he was given Leah instead of Rachel as they previously agreed. Leban's reason was that the second daughter Rachel cannot get married before the first daughter Leah, and that's why he had to give him Leah.

The bible clearly pointed out that Jacob didn't love Leah. So he had to work for Leban for another seven years in order to qualify to marry Rachel; his dream wife. That was so amazing. But something beyond Jacob was at work. That's the bloodline pattern – **a quest to marry beautiful women.**

To show that the love for beautiful women runs in Abraham's lineage, many generations after, the bible recorded in second Samuel 11:2, how David was attracted and finally took Uriah's wife because she was beautiful.

I have tried to study the four characters we have discussed above. I am still at lost why the bible emphatically stated that each married a very beautiful woman.

What is the bible trying to show us? Why must the bible tell us the kind of woman they married? Does it have to describe the kind of wife they married? Were other people's wives in the bible described as beautiful? The message is simple. The bible is showing us that they followed a pattern in their marriage.

Pattern #5
Passion for Women

David had lots of women. He had six sons in seven years by six different women, including Gentiles. And in addition to these, David had children with "his concubines" (1Chron. 3). In all, David had over 20 sons and one daughter.

Solomon took after his father. He had a greater passion for women which eventually took his life. The bible describes Solomon's downfall thus:

"King Solomon, however, loved many foreign women besides

Pharaoh's daughter –Moabites, Ammonites, Edomites, Sidonians and

Hittites.

They were from peoples which the LORD had told the

Israelites,

'You must not intermarry with them, because

they will surely turn your hearts after their gods.'

Nevertheless, Solomon held fast to them in love.

He had seven hundred wives of royal birth and three hundred

concubines,

and his wives led him astray."

(1 Kings 11:1-3 NIV)

Solomon was so crazy about women that he took the daughter of the Egyptian Pharaoh as his wife. Consequently, the numerous women Solomon associated himself with, led him astray.

From the afore-discussed examples, it is clear that some traits and patterns can run in the family or community, from one generation to another. These patterns may persist unless someone terminates it.

Chapter 4

IN ALL YOU DO, THINK OF GENERATIONS TO COME

"How blessed is the man who fears the Lord,

who greatly delights in His commandments.

His descendants will be mighty on earth;

the generation of the upright will be blessed."

(Psalm 112:1-2)

Many people selfishly live only for today. They do not understand or appreciate how one member of a family can impact other members. The fact remains that whatever we do in life (whether good or bad) has consequences and these effects trickle down to the following generations. The choices and decisions we make don't just affect us alone, but also our children, grandchildren and generations yet unborn.

Consequently, we have the ability to choose blessings or curses not only for ourselves but also for our bloodline. So, your choice matters. Your decisions today count, not only for you but for people following you.

Have you considered the saying that you never really make a choice alone? It's been said that you are always taking your parents and your children with you throughout your life.

In other words, most decisions you make are affected by the deep personal influence of your parents. On the other hand, your lifestyle, choices and major decisions will also affect future generations of your family. Consequently, it is necessary to think generationally.
Don't think of yourself alone. Think of others.

Before you undertake any venture, ask yourself, how will this affect people around me and people coming after me? Even the Scriptures often remind us that it is important to think generationally. So, even if you lack the personal desire to overcome serious problems for your own sake, do it for your family. Think generationally. Consider how any action you want to undertake will benefit or harm your descendants.

Abraham's Life Affected Generations After Him

A number of biblical passages show us why we should all think generationally. Perhaps the most striking is the example of Abraham.

Abraham was an obedient "friend of God" (James 2:23). He rejected the pagan sinful culture of his family line and chose to live a new and positive way of life. At God's request Abraham left that environment and even his own family to follow the course God set for him. In doing so, he would become known as "the father of the faithful."

Because of Abraham's willingness to abandon the sinful habits and practices of generations, God made specific promises to him about the future of his descendants. God told him, "I will make your descendants as the dust of the earth; so that if a man could number the dust of the earth, then your descendants also could be numbered" (Gen.13:16).

Recall that earlier, He had told Abraham, "I will bless those who bless you, and I will curse him who curses you; and in you all the families of the earth shall be blessed" (Genesis 12:3). About 2,000 years later, Jesus Christ; a direct descendant of Abraham was born. He died to atone for all the sins of the world and by that has purchased and is offering eternal life to all mankind. Through Jesus the son of Abraham, we have been engrafted into Abraham, and we are enjoying the Abrahamic blessings.

We are enjoying the Abrahamic blessings because Abraham, our father in faith willingly severed himself from his people and pursued a new way of life revealed to him by God. His action many years ago has affected many generations. Even those unborn who will connect to Abraham through Jesus will still enjoy the Abrahamic blessings.

David's Life Affected Many Generations After Him

Another example of a man who affected his generation is King David. Apostle Paul recorded on how God testified of David by proclaiming, "'I have found David the son of Jesse, a man after my own heart, who will do all my will."

From this man's seed, according to the promise, God raised up for Israel a Saviour - Jesus". (Acts 13:22-23) Jesus Christ was a descendant of King David, and both of them were physical descendants of Abraham. But did David's personal relationship have a positive effect on any of his other direct descendants? Did this personal relationship between God and David have benefits for David's great-grandchildren and beyond? Of course it did!

History shows that about 50 years after David's death, Judah's survival as a nation was hanging in the air. Abijah the great-grandson of King David became unfaithful to God. It is on record in the bible that he did all the same sins his father before him had done. He was not faithful to the Lord his God as David, his great-grandfather had been (1Kings 15:3).

If we are to judge swiftly, one should expect Abijah to be severely punished for his sins, and perhaps others along with him. But the bible says: "Because the Lord loved David, the Lord gave him a kingdom in Jerusalem and allowed him to have a son to be king after him. The Lord also kept Jerusalem safe" (verse 4).

The message is clear and simple. More than 50 years after David died, God showed one of his descendant's mercies because of the faithfulness of his great-grandfather!

God said in effect, "I am not doing this for you, Abijah, but because of the relationship I had with your great- grandfather David, I will show mercy unto you."
David's relationship with God also benefited many other subsequent generations. Many generations later, King Hezekiah lay dying while the nation was being threatened by

powerful Assyrian armies. The king fervently prayed to God for deliverance and the prophet Isaiah was sent to him with this message:

"Thus says the Lord, the God of David your father [ancestor]:
'I have heard your prayer,
I have seen your tears; surely I will heal you.
On the third day you shall go up to the house of the Lord.
And I will add to your days fifteen years.
I will deliver you and this city from the hand of the king of
Assyria;
and I will defend this city for My own sake, and for the sake of
my servant David'"
(2 Kings 20:5-6 emphasis mine).

Is it not very remarkable and instructive that more than 250 years after David died, God still showed mercy to his descendant? All of these were done because of David's personal relationship with God. In the scripture above, God was even proud to identify himself as the "God of David".He categorically stated that He will heal Hezekiah and protect the nation for "the sake of My servant David".

In recap, God was simply saying: "Hezekiah, I am not doing this just for your sake! I am doing it because of my relationship with your ancestor David."

Can you see how powerful and impactful an individual's actions can be on his or her descendants for generations?

You can be the Abraham or David in your family. You can set a pattern that may bless your descendant and generations from now.

Jonathan Edwards's Life Affected His Descendants

Apart from the many examples we have read from the Holy Book, many other examples abound to show how powerful generational influences of parents can be on their own family and descendants. Another significant example is a man called Jonathan Edward. Jonathan Edwards was a famous preacher who was born in 1703. He was a deeply religious man who lived a life of strong moral values. In addition to being a preacher, he was a dedicated family man. He was married to a very religious woman named Sarah, who shared his values, and they had eleven children. He was so successful that he later became the president of Princeton University.

A study carried out by Winship on 1,400 descendants of Jonathan and Sarah Edward by 1874, reveals the following:

- 13 were college presidents.

- 65 were college professors.

- 100 were attorneys.

- 32 were state judges.

- 85 were authors of classic books.

- 66 were physicians.

- 80 held political offices, including three state governors.

- 3 were state senators.

- 1 became vice president of the United States.

Wow! What a generation! It's amazing how a father's blessings produced amazing results in the life of his descendants. The seeds of Jonathan Edwards received not only financial blessings but also the supernatural blessings. May such be your testimony in Jesus name, Amen!

You Can Affect Your Generation Negatively

It should be made categorically clear that inasmuch as one generation can affect the other positively, it can as well affect them negatively.

For example, in 1874, a member of the New York State Prison Board, noticed that six members of the same family were incarcerated at the same time. The board did a research on this family.

They looked back at a few generations in the bid to unravel the original couple who initiated this tragic family legacy and they traced the family line back to their ancestor born in 1720, a man considered lazy and godless with a reputation as the town troublemaker. He was also an alcoholic and viewed as an individual with no morals. To make matters worse, he married a woman who had similar flaws like he did, and together they had six daughters and two sons.

Here is what the report revealed about the approximately 1,200 descendants of this couple who were alive by 1874:

- 310 were homeless
- 160 were prostitutes.
- 180 suffered from drug or alcohol abuse.
- 150 were criminals who spent time in prison (including 7, who were charged with murder).

The report also found that the State of New York had spent $1.5 million - a shockingly high number at the time – to care for this line of descendants, and not one had made a significant contribution to society.

Sadly, we can see by this example how the harmful dysfunctions of parents can be passed down from generation to generations.

Chapter 5

DIFFERENT FORMS OF NEGATIVE BLOODLINE PATTERNS

"Both thorns and thistles it shall bring forth for you,

And you shall eat the herb of the field.

In the sweat of your face you shall eat bread till you return to

the ground,

For out of it you were taken; For dust you are,

And to dust you shall return."

(GEN 3:18-19 NKJV)

Before you can deal effectively with negative generational patterns, you need to identify what they look like. We have discussed in previous chapters some forms of family negative patterns. It is remarkable to note that having one of these in your life or family may not necessarily indicate a family plague. However, to have several forms of these incidences "reoccurring" in your life or lineage could be an index to a pattern. The help of the Holy Spirit is vital in identifying a family pattern. As we study the different forms of family negative patterns, ask the Holy Spirit to open your eyes to identify areas of dysfunctional patterns in your family.

#1 Family Sicknesses

Some family negative patterns manifest in the form of sicknesses. How do you describe the situation where many people in a family suffer the same kind of sickness, or die of the same kind of disease? This could be cancer, diabetes, Asthma, arthritis, madness, inflammations and sicknesses of all kinds.

Science have come up with terminologies to describe this ailments, Some of which have been attributed to hereditary. But whether it has a natural or spiritual root; we still brand it a "negative pattern" due to its re-occurrence in families that is manifested in the form of sickness.

Why should you die of what your father died of? Do you have the same destiny? Is that the will of God for you?

God never intends that members of the same family should suffer and die of the same health challenge.

The Testimony That Opened My Eyes

August 27, 2012, will remain indelible to me. I walked out of the church auditorium with deep sense of satisfaction, after about three hours of ministration. I was a guest speaker at a youth program organized by a pastor who happens to be a close associate. After experiencing the great move of God in the midst of His people that day, I assured myself, "No man who attended this service should ever complain of any problem again. Every mountain has been crushed, every valley filled and all embargos uplifted". All I expected from everyone who attended that program was testimonies.

My expectations were not cut short. Few days after the program, the pastor called to inform me that numerous testimonies have been received since we had that program. Some people who succeeded in getting my phone number called me to testify of God's touch. I was shocked how one of the callers ended her own testimony. She came with a swollen leg to the service, God touched her, and she became normal two days after the program.

She termed it a miracle. She said to me: "God has delivered me for this year. Man of God, please permit me to make a request in advance. Before next year's trouble starts, I will come and meet you for prayers."

I was lost at first. I didn't really understand the meaning of "before next year's case starts..." So I asked to find out what she meant. She then told me that every year, between September and December, her two legs get swollen, and she will be in deep pains. Within this period of the year, her family takes her to several hospitals in search of cure. A lot of monies are usually spent, and on two occasions, she had been taken outside the country for treatment. She had gone to many prayer houses for spiritual healing, coupled with various kinds of medications. Most times, the problem relapses, only to resurface the following year, at exactly the same time of the year. So to say, the problem reoccurs every year. There is an established pattern. The woman knows this. She is just convinced that she will have such problem every year.

After her story, I was provoked in the spirit and I declared that the miracle will remain permanent. Glad to say that since then, she has never experienced that problem again.

After her healing, she has brought two of her siblings to our prayer meetings, and I discovered that members of that family suffers similar ailments. The problem is that medical science has no explanation for the sickness and laboratory tests reveals nothing.

The reoccurring bloodline pattern in the afore-mentioned family is swollen leg sickness. However, many other bloodline patterns could exist such as cancer and other forms of diseases in some other families. This is what we term, bloodline patterns.

#2 Barrenness, Impotence, Female Problems

The first mandate God gave to man is:
"…Be fruitful and increase in number,
fill the earth and subdue it…"
(Gen.1: 28 NIV).

All through the Old Testament, the commandment, "Be fruitful and increase…" was repeated 18 times in the New International Version (NIV)) of the bible. By this commission, man was elevated to the status of a co-creator with God. What an honour and privilege! But God did not just stop at giving man the mandate to procreate. In His infinite wisdom; He put in man everything needful to realize this mandate. In the man He put the 'sperm' which is the seed of procreation and in the woman the 'ovum' or the egg. It is important to categorically state that it is the mind of God that every man or woman should be capable of carrying out this divine assignment of fruitfulness and multiplication. Hence He promised in the bible:

"You shall be blessed above all peoples;
there shall not be male or female barren among you
or among your cattle"
(Deut. 7:14 AMP).

Another scripture puts it this way:

"And none will miscarry or be barren in your land…"
(Ex. 23: 26 NIV).

To paraphrase, the two scriptures are simply saying: "All of you will be able to procreate. None of you will suffer infertility.

Every man among you will be able to impregnate his wife and every woman will be able to conceive". God even included our livestock as things that will never suffer barrenness.

God loves fruitfulness (Mk.11:14, Lk. 13:7-8).

Unfortunately, some men and women lack the capability to carry out this assignment. Thus, they are tagged 'infertile'; a name God assured that none of His children will be identified with. The number of people plagued with infertility is becoming increasingly alarming.

Some of the causal factors of infertility in men are low sperm count, inability of sperm to swim, sexually transmitted diseases   (STDs), erectile dysfunction, etc. In women, it comes in form of infections, hormonal problems, menstrual problems, fibroids, miscarriages, etc.

Sometimes, most of the afore-listed fertility challenges become a reoccurring decimal in a family lineage.

I once heard a story of a family where three girls of the same mother got married to different men but none of them could conceive after many years of marriage. There is also another family where men hardly come to marry ladies there. The allegation is that ladies from that family hardly give birth normally except via caesarean operations. There is also another family where more than 90% of the men there usually lack the ability to impregnate their wives. Their wives usually get pregnant via the services of an outsider. All these can be adjudged as negative patterns that need to be broken.

#3 Peculiar Family Sin

The first time I went to the police station to bail somebody was in 2004. One of our brothers in the fellowship was arrested, and on hearing that, we rushed to the police to ensure his release.

"This guy is an honest man and cannot commit the crime you are accusing him of", we told the police. One of the police men asked us, "Are you sure of what you are saying? Do you really know this guy?" "Yes we do", we answered him.

He then called me aside and said to me: "Be careful how you involve yourself in this case because this guy comes from an uncultured home with no good records.

They are thieves. It runs in their blood. He is a strong suspect, and until our investigations prove otherwise, we will not free him. So I will advise that you allow the police to do their work".

Wow! The words, "He comes from an uncultured home..." put me off balance and I lost the confidence to defend him any further.

Few years ago, I was privileged to counsel a man who could not explain why he was an addicted swindler. Though he claimed to be a devoted Christian, he was a fraud. He maximized every little opportunity to defraud anyone who comes in contact with him. He couldn't understand why it was so. He had resolved to stop it, made so many resolutions year after year, but whenever he was financially broke, that nature shows up and he finds himself defrauding someone.

During the course of our discussions, I tried to unravel if his behavior was consequent upon environmental influences, or any psychological disorder. But the truth is that his condition was neither   psychologically nor environmentally ignited.

I discovered that his father, brothers and even few of his uncles have all been involved in financial crimes at one time or the other. In fact, his younger brother was recently picked up by the police for stealing his neighbour's cell phone. I made him understand that it was not a coincidence that many people in his family are involved in fraud. There is a negative pattern that needs to be dealt with.

The take away from this story is that some sins run in the bloodline. Over the years, this message has sunk deeper because of abounding evidence.

If you check well within your locality, there are some families that are known for a particular kind of sin or evil, such that once you mention the name of that family, everyone who knows them will easily associate them with that evil. For example, there are families that are known for their lifestyle of stealing. Some are known for sexual promiscuity, murder, lies, amongst others.

#4 Family Breakdowns and Divorces

Some families have high proclivity for divorce. In some, you find deep rooted divisions, fights, quarrels and enmity among family members. Most times, even when some people in such families consciously try hard to avoid such vices and misfortunes, they find themselves unknowingly and irresistibly aligning with such bloodline patterns. The spirits responsible for these patterns fight hard to ensure their assignments come to pass.

How do you explain a situation where in an extended family, more than six people are in jail? And in their history, many people in that family have been jailed. Do you think it is normal? No! There is an active evil pattern at play.

In 2014, a woman shared a story with me on how hard she fought never to be entrapped in the net of divorce that runs in their family lineage. Her three elder sisters were divorcees. She attributed her sisters' failures in marriage to bad choices of partners.

So, before she got married, she resolved to be very careful never to fall into the hands of a "wrong man".

God blessed her with a very good man, and to the best of her ability, she played her part as a good wife.

For some time, the marriage was going on fine. Convinced and carried away by the strong and true love between her and the husband, she felt that nothing on earth would ever lead to break up in her marriage. But in 2011, she joined the league of single mothers in her family. How did this happen? Her husband was posted to Ghana for official duties. He spent 6 years there, though he was visiting home once in a while. The woman could not relocate with him because of her own job.

Unfortunately, the man was lured into amorous life by a Ghanaian woman, and the woman got pregnant for him. Within a space of time they had two children.

Upon hearing this, she was furious and could not stomach such ignoble act. This resulted to serious issues in the family. Friends and relatives tried to intervene but to no avail. Finally, they separated and she joined the league of divorcees in the family lineage.

You can see that the gravity of love she lavished on the man, and the scrupulous and painstaking selection process for the so called 'right man' did not save her from joining the league of single mothers in her family lineage.

It wasn't the woman's fault, neither was the man happy with what happened. But the fact is that a spiritual force was at work to ensure that the negative pattern of 'marry and divorce' that was operational in the family was adhered to. Spiritual forces that fuel divorce ensure that people who labour under this pattern do not last in marriage. Their assignment is to make sure marriages crumble. In fact, sometimes, when the spirit fails to activate a divorce, he may resort to take either the husband or wife away by sudden death, just to ensure that the pattern of being single even after marriage is enforced.

Just as families suffer negative patterns in some areas, some nations also have some forms of negative patterns they are known for. Research has shown that some nations suffer this negative pattern of divorce than others.

For example, a report released by Forest Institute of Professional Psychology shows that the divorce rate in America is 50% for first marriages, 67% for second marriages and 74% for third marriages. In Japan, the divorce rate is 27%, Singapore 10%, and India 1%. From the statistics above, you can see that the reoccurrence of divorce in America is higher than that of India. So to say, it is riskier to marry an American than an Indian.

#5 Lack, Poverty and Indebtedness

Lack and poverty seem to be the most common negative pattern prevalent in many families especially in the developing world. Arguably, most people will claim that these problems are attributable to bad governance in some nations. But most times, it is a curse.

The bible concurs that poverty could be as a result of curses. See what the book of Deuteronomy says:

"Cursed shall be thy basket and thy store." **(Deut. 28:17)**
"...and thou shalt not prosper in thy ways:
and thou shalt be only oppressed and spoiled evermore,
and no man shall save thee." **(Deut. 28:29)**

People under this pattern never have good savings. Their ability to get wealth is restricted. They are continually oppressed by bill collectors, and the little they dare to accumulate is soon stolen by the spoilers. They work like elephant but eat like grasshopper. They feed from hand to mouth.

A person under this pattern will squander, waste and get further into debt and bondage. They are candidates for get-rich schemes of all kinds. Poverty simply means not having what you need to do God's will and it always leads to indebtedness. Suffice it to mention that it is not the will of God that you should not have the necessary means to accomplish His plans for your life. These family patterns of 'Lack and Poverty' need to be broken because it is not the will of God.

How do I know this? See what the Holy book says:

"And God is able to make all grace abound toward you;

that ye, always having all sufficiency in all things,

may abound to every good work".

(2 Cor. 9:8)

"For you know the grace of our Lord Jesus Christ,

that though he was rich, yet for your sake he became poor,

so that you through his poverty might become rich".

(2 Cor. 8:9 NIV)

#6 No Ambition, No Vision, No Direction

Ambition can be defined as a strong desire to make a difference with your life. It is the vision, dream, or aspiration to succeed.

Normally, people show some level of ambition and push hard to succeed in whatever they do. They take pains and resist the storms of life in pursuit of their dreams.

Unfortunately, there are families where people care less about tomorrow. They are without ambition. They go aimlessly through life. They are without hope and terribly negative.

They "grope" as "blind men" with no direction. They have no internal vision for their lives. They set no goals and are blown to and fro by life's circumstances. This is not normal.

Well, it could be trivialized when just one person is involved. But when a lot of people in the family are manifesting such attitudes and are struggling aimlessly to survive, it could be suspected that there is a curse running through the family that needs to be broken.

> "And you shall grope at noonday,
> as the blind gropes in darkness,
> and you shall not prosper in your ways:
> and you shall be only oppressed and spoiled ever more,
> and no man shall save you" **(Deut. 28:29)**

#7 Emotional Instability and Fear

Family negative patterns can be in the form of emotional instability such as, insanity, craziness, foolishness, senseless behaviour and flakiness. It can also come as the spirit of confusion, indecision, fear, inferiority complex, depression and wonderment. These are easily overcome by emotions and fear and thus triggers a person to make foolish decisions and do crazy or self-destructive things. In this condition, a person has a continual inner struggle, internal warfare and frustration.

Such bloodline pattern informs why some are double-minded and have problems ordering their lives with the word of God and renewing their minds.

#8 Bondage and Slavery

Some negative patterns are in form of bondage and enslavement. A person under this influence loses his individualism, liberty and freedom. Such persons are easily controlled and manipulated into loss of identity and personal liberties, which affects their abilities to make decisions without getting permission from their masters.

This people will look to other gods for provision and protection, not unto the Lord. They are faithless, carnal, and full of idolatry, entertainment and anything that divides them from the Lordship of Christ.

#9 Drop Out Syndrome

Some years back, I had a friend called Kola who had no intention of going to the university. After much persuasion from some of his friends, he reluctantly wrote entrance exams and surprisingly got admission into the university. Unlike most of us, he was never excited that he got admission because he felt it was unnecessary. His father was a business tycoon. All he wanted was to continue in his father's footsteps.

After the second year in the university, Kola withdrew without any cogent reason. Anyways, I was not shocked, because from his immediate to extended family; no one had ever crossed secondary school level.

His father had five children, few that attempted going to school dropped out along the line. The situation is not normal. It is evident that a negative pattern called 'Drop out syndrome' is at work in that family.

#10 Marrying Many Wives

A colleague in the office once shared a story of the bloodline pattern that was operational in his extended family. According to him, men in their family are renowned for marrying multiple wives. His great grandfather married six women, his grandfather married three, his four uncles have married more than one wife or have children from more than one woman and most of his cousins also toed that line. In fact, three of his cousins have had children with different women.

To his chagrin, his father; well lettered and acclaimed to be a very strong believer has just married for the third time. He divorced his mother who was the first wife. Recently the second wife left for reasons unknown to anyone, and the man was left with no option than to marry another woman, making it the third wife. Such lifestyle is not ordinary. It is orchestrated by demonic influences. Such forces fight marriages and ensure it crumbles.

Have You Discovered Your Peculiar Bloodline Pattern?

Any man that is not aware of the pattern that functions in his family is in a terrible and pitiable situation, because Satan will use it against him.

I have seen families that have a pattern of laziness and yet are not aware that being lazy in their family has been a generational pattern that has been dominant in the family from time immemorial. The devil over the years had used laziness to keep the family in penury.

I have seen a family where almost every young man there impregnates at least one girl in the neighborhood before marriage and they don't see anything ignoble about such act. They just see it as being 'sharp', 'being man enough', etc.

Some people are permanently limited to one level of life. Some can never get married until they become pregnant. In some families, women control their husbands. The examples are too many to mention. Knowing the pattern that functions in your own bloodline is very important. It will help you to know how to strategically channel your fight.

Chapter 6

SOME FACTORS THAT IGNITE NEGATIVE BLOODLINE PATTERNS

"Please inquire of past generations,

And consider the things searched out by their fathers."

(Job 8:8)

"If the foundations be destroyed, what can the righteous do?"

(Psalms 11:3)

The bible says: "A curse without a cause cannot stand"(Prov. 26:2).That is to say: "Things don't just happen". Something certainly gives negative patterns legal rights to operate in a person's life or bloodline.

The bible and life experiences give us clues to possible causal factors of negative bloodline patterns.

#1 The Sin Factor

"Render unto them a recompense, O LORD, according to the

work of their hands.

Give them sorrow of heart, thy curse unto them.

Persecute and destroy them in anger
From under the heavens of the LORD."
(Lam. 3:64-66)

The bible passage above teaches that sorrows and life's troubles could sometimes be as a result of people's evil deeds. The pattern has not changed. People still reap what they sowed. A young man once sought to have a quick confab with me. I obliged him in accordance with the demands of my calling. During our talk, he passionately narrated a bloodline pattern that has been in operation in their family for a very long time. In fact, as at the time of our encounter, his elder brother was still held in the web of that pattern. According to his story, there is a popular river in their village. Before the advent of Christianity, the villagers used to worship the goddess of this river. In fact, even currently, some people who have not given their lives to Christ still worship this water spirit. It is believed that this spirit does all kinds of favours to those who seek her assistance.

According to their custom, once the river goddess answers your prayers, you are expected to carry out some prayers and rituals at the river yearly in order to sustain the so called blessings. Non adherence to these conditions usually attracts some repercussions.

According to him, the great grandmother received some favours from the so- called goddess. In obedience to the demands of the culture, she visited the river for the yearly rituals in appreciation of the goddess. She was faithful in doing so for many years. However, after some years she began to vacillate and relent in her usual one year visitations and rituals at the river. This was the genesis of her problems. She started having all forms of life threatening problems including health challenges. Few times she fell into coma and eventually lost her life in a shameful manner.

Stories had it that from that time on, every first son of that lineage faced serious strange health problems. Even his eldest brother was seriously down with a strange sickness as at the time we met.

After series of counselling and preparatory prayers, we scheduled an appointment with the family members. We led them to genuine repentance and confession of their sins, ministered the word to them and broke the negative pattern by the reason of the anointing. That terminated the dominion of the evil one and the circle of sickness in that family.

From the narratives above, the genesis of this family's problems was sin of idol worshipping, and immediately the sin factor was treated, freedom became possible and the devil's influences were given quit notice.

Sin can open the way for the devil into a man's life or that of his family. It gives the devil the legal right to operate anyhow, anywhere and at any time in your life or family. And if the devil can have his way in your life, you will definitely run at a loss with everything turning out bad.

When God comes into a place, He comes with His luggage – blessings, healing, salvation, peace, etc. Likewise when the devil comes into a place, he comes with his properties – sickness, poverty and curses.

Suffice it to mention that some bad experiences a lot of families suffer today are probably because someone along the generational line gave the devil the license or effrontery to come in. That license could be a sinful act. So to say, it doesn't necessarily have to be your own sins that may attract negative pattern in your life or family. Someone up the family tree could be the cause for a generational affliction. Sins committed in the past by family ancestors might attract some consequences, which could be what the future generation is suffering.

In other words, negative bloodline pattern characterized with afflictions, poverty and failures could be a payment or "recompense for iniquity." Unfortunately, you cannot choose your relatives, just as you cannot choose your skin colour, gender, or race. Once you are born into any family, you share in their life experiences, blessings or curses.

Some sins are too abominable that they attract weightier curses. Most times, the effects of the sin pass down to the lineage of the person who committed the evil, thus, negative patterns are created. The bible has some remarkable examples to buttress this stand point.

In Genesis 38:15-18, Judah, one of the sons of Jacob opened the door to Satan when he committed incest with her daughter in-law Tamar. That incestuous relationship produced an illegitimate son named Perez. God was displeased with this and that singular act of evil deprived Judah's legitimate lineage the throne for ten generations.

Why was it so? The simple answer is because Judah sinned against God. Recall that the bible has already made a pronouncement that:

"A bastard shall not enter into the congregation of the Lord; even to his tenth generation shall he not enter into the congregation of the Lord."   (Deut.28:2)

In fulfilment to the biblical predictions and prescriptions, it took ten generations (between Perez and David) for a son from the legitimate lineage of Judah to regain the throne.

Judah begot Perez and Zerah by Tamar,
Perez begot Hezron,
And Hezron begot Ram.
Ram begot Amminadab,
Amminadab begot Nahshon,
and Nahshon begot Salmon.
Salmon begot Boaz by Rahab
Boaz begot Obed by Ruth,
Obed begot Jesse,
And Jesse begot David the King."
(Matthew 1:3-6 NKJV)

So, if your family is passing through rough times consistently, incongruent with the blessings of God prescribed in the scriptures for believers, take your time, reflect and ask yourself, "Have we gone wrong anywhere?" The sin factor could be the problem.

#2 Curses and Negative Pronouncements

Someone of superior authority like your parents, your pastor, your leaders in various places and institutions and also people you have offended may curse you, and this may trigger a negative pattern in your life and family until it is terminated.

Pastor Cursed Thieves

I once heard a story of some young men who went to a church and stole some musical and media equipment. The pastor of the church got angry because this has been happening to the church for a long time. Each time it happens, the church will simply overlook and replace the stolen equipment. But this time, the church felt the thieves were taken them and their God for granted. So, the pastor demanded that whoever stole those properties should return them within seven days.

After seven days, the properties were not returned. The pastor got angry and pronounced a curse on those responsible for the stealing. Three weeks later, the leader of the gang died in a mysterious circumstance. In the 5th week, two other members of the gang were involved in an accident that consumed their lives. In the 7th week, the body of the last member of the group was found dead in a nearby bush in the village. As if that wasn't enough, each of those families lost a child within 6 months of that pronouncement. In the 8th month, another child of the gang leader died.

Alarmed by the incessant deaths and other unfathomable calamities these families were experiencing, the wife of one of the men involved in the robbery; who was privy to all the stealing in church rushed to the pastor and confessed, and apologized on behalf of her family. The other families were also gathered, and they apologized on behalf of their husbands cum father. The church forgave them and the pastor prayed for them, and the calamities that were visiting them ceased.

An Old Woman Cursed A Raper

A couple of years back, a young man of about 18 years of age raped an old woman coming back from the farm. The elderly woman had serious bleeding after the encounter. She wept profusely and angrily placed a curse on these boy and his generation. She said thus: "Since you have no respect for an old woman, your family will never have an old man or woman".

It sounded trivial and negligible but it was loaded with power. Some years after, this guy got married, had children, but died before he was 40 years old. It was also discovered that no one crosses 40 years in the family. Their children were dying prematurely. It took a young man in the family who got a revelation of the causes of the calamity to put a stop to the untimely death pattern erupted by his grandfather. This he did by asking for forgiveness on behalf of his ancestor and pronouncing freedom by the blood of Jesus to the family and normalcy was restored. When people (especially those who have superior authority over you) curse or make any form of negative pronouncement against you, don't trivialize it because there is power in spoken words. Ensure you cancel it, and if necessary, make them reverse what they have said.

#3 Family Altars

"If the foundations be destroyed,
what can the righteous do?"
(Psalm11:3)

Every family has an altar, each family has some idiosyncrasies and every family is governed by a spirit. It could be a positive spirit (God's Spirit) or a negative spirit (demons). There is no neutral ground. There is no family without a spiritual governor.

If your earthly home is ruled and controlled by a demon, there will certainly be some negative patterns that will be prevalent in your family. Similarly if it is controlled by the Spirit of the living God, positive things will be happening in your family.

Family altar here does not necessarily imply physical altar, although it may also be involved. Family altar refers to God or the god that is served in your family.

An altar is a place of sacrifice, and sacrifices are made to gods. It depends however on the god that is served on that altar. If a family chooses to serve the living God, the altar of the living God will be their place of sacrifice in that family. If however they choose to serve other gods (demons), altars of these lower gods will be established in their homes.

The altar in your family determines what happens to your family. The altar of the almighty, most merciful, ever loving and good doing God will attract God's blessings and favour. Similarly, the altar of the wicked and evil spirits will attract evil to your family. A food for thought is, what altar exists in my family?

Evil altars will attract premature deaths, failure, divorce, poverty, sickness, and many other evil things. In fact, whenever you see these negative happenstances predominating the lifestyles and experiences of a family, know that an evil altar is at work. It is pertinent to ask your family elders questions as regards how your elders served or worshipped in the past.

The knowledge of what transpired in your family will help you know what you are dealing with, so as to know how to channel your fight of faith and warfare prayers.

#4 Ancestral and Territorial Spirits

The destinies of nations, communities and families are determined first in the spiritual realm before they manifest in the physical. The spiritual controls the physical. Viewing life issues from the natural alone will certainly give you an off beam perception of how destinies are controlled.

There are ancestral spirits that fight to control the way events unfold in families. There are also territorial spirits that strive to control the people living in a certain region. For example, there are some communities in Nigeria that are renowned for providing others with servants, gardeners and house helps. If you want a nanny in the country, there are some states in the country your mind will first of all go to.

The reason is, there are territorial spirits that seemingly control people's mind, desires and aspirations in those regions. Such territorial spirits make them to have the mindset of servitude.

Negative powers do incalculable and intense battles to thwart the destinies of God's children. Their intent is to ensure that God's divine plans for His children do not come to fruition.

Lesson from Daniel's Encounter

The most common example of a battle for the destiny of a nation is found in Daniel chapter 10. According to the scriptures, Daniel fasted and prayed for 21 days for Israel. God in response to his prayers sent an Angel to bring answers to Daniel. But the Angel was withheld in the air by a demon known as the prince of Persia. It took Michael the Archangel to battle with the demon and clear the way for the Angel with the message from God to reach Daniel.

It is remarkable to note that Daniel's prayers was heard from the first day he prayed. But a territorial spirit stopped the angel with the answers in the air. Certainly this spirit never wanted Israel to enjoy the goodies from their father in heaven. Persia was the most powerful kingdom amongst every other kingdom at that time with about one hundred and seventy provinces. Of course, the demon that is recognized as the prince of a powerful empire will have to be powerful.

After delivering the message to Daniel, the Angel went further to say that he was going back to join Michael in the fight and that after that, he was going to fight the prince of Greece.

A salient revelation in this scripture is that there are many battles going on in the spiritual realm regarding the destinies of nations.

Satan has a structure of angelic beings over every nation, country, city and even families. He is the god of this world, and one of his assignments is to thwart people's destinies from God's plans. God's plans and desires for His children are for good; to bring us into an expected end (Jer. 29:11).

Chapter 7

CAN A BELIEVER BE AFFECTED BY NEGATIVE FAMILY PATTERNS?

"And not only they, but ourselves also,

which have the first fruits of the spirit,

even we ourselves groan within ourselves,

waiting for the adoption, to wit, the redemption of our body."

(Rom 8:23)

During a counseling session in one of our office days, a man who claimed to have been born again for over five years asked me: "Man of God, even after being born again, can I still be under the influence of family negative patterns?" I ask because I don't understand what is happening to me. Why am I still passing through similar situations with some of my siblings who are not yet born again?

I prayed to the Holy Spirit for divine wisdom to handle his matter appropriately. I then asked him, "If things were moving well in the family; that is to say, if the patterns of events are positive, would you like to continue to enjoy the blessings? For example, if you enjoy good health, long life and prosperity in your family, would you like to have a share of these goodies even though you have become born again? Or would you like to be cut off from every good thing that pertains to your family just because you are now born again?" He kept mute for some time and later answered, "Who doesn't like good things? I will like to enjoy the goodies with my family."

Then I said to him, That you are now born again does not separate or deny you of all the blessings your family enjoys. You don't necessarily have to change your surname because you are now born again, neither does your DNA change because you are born again. Your name is not erased from your father's Will because you claim to be a new creation. You have a claim of a portion of your father's properties because you still carry his blood. Though you now belong to Christ, you are still part of your physical family. What affects them affects you too. You share their joy, pains, and sadness, among many other outcomes.

Your Family Battles and Challenges Will Still Confront You

The patterns, blames, debts and troubles that are associated with your family will always want to identify with you. Being born again will not immune you to the challenges that are associated with your family. For example, if your father was indebted to someone or a bank before he died, you will not say because you are now born again, your father's debtors should not bother you. No! You have to pay because it is part of the things you inherited. Just as a man who loses his father would want all his father's debtors to pay him all the debts owed his late father, he should also be prepared to honour his father's creditors when they come knocking. You don't inherit only the good things, you also inherit the challenges. But how you manage the challenges is up to you.

A negative bloodline pattern is simply the effect of curses that are still running in the bloodline. A curse on its own cannot enforce itself. It takes a demon to ensure a curse is effectual. So even when someone has experienced the new birth, the demon sent to police the curse still tends to work. It becomes your responsibility to shut the door that was opened in the past.

To understand why many Christians still labour under some family negative patterns even after they have been born again, we need to understand the concept of salvation.

Different Stages of Salvation

Man is a spirit with a soul that lives in a body. Succinctly put, man is made up of spirit, soul and body. Suffice it to say that the salvation package which Jesus delivered to man is a complete package. All the three ingredients of a complete man were put into consideration. None was left out in God's divine plan. For ease in explanation, we can say that salvation is in three folds:

The salvation of the spirit

The salvation of the soul

The salvation of the body

Stage 1.
The Salvation of the Spirit Man

The moment you accept and confess the Lordship of Jesus Christ over your life, something happens to your spirit man.

> "Therefore if any man be in Christ,
> he is a new creature: old things are passed away;
> behold all things are become new". **(2 Cor. 5:17)**

All things being new as stated in this chapter has nothing to do with your outward man but the inward man. You need to understand that it was not the outward man that got saved immediately you confessed the Lordship of Jesus over your life, but the inward man; which is the spirit man.

For example, your complexion will not change; character flaws will not change instantaneously at the point of confessing Jesus as your Lord and saviour the day you got born again. The outward man remains the same. Even the soulish realms where man's mind and emotions are will not be affected instantaneously during the new birth experience. The salvation of these aspects of man is not automatic, but comes gradually.

Stage 2.

The Salvation of Your Soul

When you got saved, every problem you had in your soul was still there. The betrayals you had in the past and the quest for vengeance is still very much in your soul.

How then is man's soul saved? Apostle Paul in his epistle to the Romans tells us how. He teaches that our minds needs to be transformed by the renewing of the mind. (Rom 12:2)

This means we need the repairing, the restoration and the healing of the soul by the word of God for the soul to be saved. For the soul to be saved, it will take personal effort, personal discipline, and spiritual intensity and commitment to the word of God to be achieved.

So your spirit can be born again and you can be blood washed, but act as unsaved because the soul remains unsaved and canal. Until the mind is renewed, the soul is still the same.

Stage 3
The Salvation of the Body

The third and of course, the consummation of man's salvation is the salvation of the body. This will only be fully realized on the resurrection morning. According to the bible, this mortal body will become immortal, and this corruptible and inglorious body will become incorruptible and glorious after the resurrection.

The Implication of Different Levels of Salvation

We have established that the salvation of the spirit man happens automatically immediately you confess the Lordship of Jesus over your life. But the other two stages of salvation happen gradually afterwards.

While these two aspects of human salvation are still in process, man will still be battling with the challenges associated with the fallen man. That is why the body can still die, get sick or wounded. That is why you can get angry or have bad thoughts even after you are born again.

A genuinely born again Christian cannot house a demon in his spirit. In other words, a demon cannot attack his spirit man once he becomes born again. This is so because his spirit has been recreated by the Holy Spirit. He is now a new creation according to 2nd Corinthians 5:17. According to the scriptures, the recreated Christian's spirit becomes the dwelling place of the Holy Spirit (John 14:23; 1Cor.6:17), and thus, cannot also be the dwelling place of an evil spirit
(2 Cor. 6:14-16; James 3:11-12).

However, a demon can intermittently attack a person's soul or body since these components of man have not been fully saved. As we have learnt earlier, the salvation of these components of man comes gradually.

In recap, a Christian can be oppressed or obsessed in BODY or SOUL by a demon but certainly his spirit cannot be touched. This explains why after being born again, a Christian can still experience some negative things some unbelievers in his family experiences except he stands his ground as a believer and deals with them. Curses, diseases, misfortunes, wicked habits and immoral characters have influences over one's body and soul and not over the spirit man.

These vices and negative patterns are transmitted in the family from generation to generation. It is totally up to any born again Christian to deal with whatever was transmitted to him or her before the new birth, by the reprogramming, healing and transformation of his soul through the application of the word of God in the area that it is needed.

We must learn how to let our spirit - our inner man rule over the body. It will solve so many issues regarding the pattern in the family we find ourselves.

Most times, our problems are not necessarily the strength of the curse or demonic activity, but man's flesh dominating the recreated human spirit. Keeping the body subject to the spirit is the major work of every believer after the new birth. Although this may not be achieved over night, it is mandatory if you want to shut the road permanently and lock out the enemy.

Lessons from Lazarus Resurrection

In John 11, Jesus was called upon by Mary and Martha when Lazarus was sick. Unfortunately, before he arrived, Lazarus was already dead for 4 days. Jesus came and commanded Lazarus to come out of the grave. He came out, but was still bound with the grave clothes.

Notice this carefully. Lazarus had life in him after he was raised from the dead by the power of Jesus Christ. But he was still bound up by the grave clothes. Put in another way, Lazarus was living but still bound up with grave clothes. The deduction here is that there are people who are saved; who really love the Lord, and they are sitting in different churches listening to the gospel being preached but they are still wearing grave clothes. They are still bound up with old habits.

They are still bound up with works of the flesh. In other words, the smell of death is still on them although they claim to have accepted Christ and are following him.

Examples of Family Patterns Some Believers Still Experience

He Beats His Wife Though Born Again

A woman came to our office in Lagos with tears and bruises all over her body. She narrated how her husband gave her the beatings of her life after a short argument.

The man in question was a worker in one of the churches in town. They've been having some family issues. All the efforts by her local church authority to settle the matter proved abortive. We were taken aback to hear that a born again brother could deal with his wife with such callosity.

Upon enquiry, we came to discover that the man has been beating this woman even before they became born again. In fact, he has always battered any woman he has been in relationship with. Unfortunately, he continued with this act even after he claimed to have been born again. The worst is that he can't even explain why he batters his wife. In spite of many resolutions and decisions, he finds himself repeating this old habit. Each time after beating his wife, he will simply say: "I don't know what came over me".

We later discovered that his father used to beat his mother, and his grandfather did the same. In fact, information has it that his elder brother also beats his wife.

Will you say the man is not born again? Of course he is. He confessed the Lordship of Jesus over his life and his spirit man has been born again, but he has to pass through the process of having his mind being gradually renewed.

He doesn't enjoy beating his wife. He knows that a real believer shouldn't do that. But that is a family pattern he has to deal with. Being born again is an instant incident, but renewal of the mind is a gradual process.

Born Again Yet Barren

I know three sisters of the same parents who gave their lives to Christ several years ago. I can attest that they are genuine believers and are members of the prayer band of their respective churches, yet they are yet to conceive. All medical help has proven abortive.

How do you describe their situation? Can you allude that they are not genuinely born again because they are childless? No! This has nothing to do with their spirit man being born again. It simply has to do with a bad pattern in the family (as regards their health) that has to be dealt with.

Born Again But Still Sick

There is a family where 90% of the members use eye glasses, including the pastors among them. There is also another one where almost everybody has tooth problem including those in church. Another family has members who predominantly suffer ulcer. One of my friends happen to come from this family and always avoid long fasting because of the challenge of ulcer. I also know of another family where almost everybody who died there died of cancer. If being born again alone is enough to terminate such bloodline pattern, then most of them should have no reason to complain.

Born Again But Still Poor

The commonest bloodline pattern you can find in church today is poverty. More than 90% of the people who come to church are poverty stricken and beggarly.

In church today, you will find people whose great grandfathers, grand fathers and fathers were poor and they themselves are suffering from serious poverty. Does it mean that they are not genuinely born again? No! They may be faithful believers. The problem is not solved by being born again alone, but the poverty cycle that has to be broken when you begin to apply some kingdom principles and protocols and learning to work hard and smart.

Born Again But Anger Still Reigns

In my village, there is a family that is popularly known for their extreme anger. Despite the fact that many of them claim to be born again, anger still dominates their behaviours. Stories have it that even their grandparents were known for their extreme anger.

The message here is that it is still possible to be born again and still pass through some of the challenges other members of your family are passing through.

Chapter 8

HOW TO DEAL WITH NEGATIVE PATTERNS

"Behold, I have given you authority to tread on serpents and

scorpions,

and over all the power of the enemy,

and nothing will injure you".

(LUKE 10:19)

As a matter of fact, every man or woman on earth has some issues that are connected to family lineage he or she is battling with. Sometimes we have to confront problems that originated many generations ago. It may not be your fault, but there is a demand upon you to halt and obliterate it from your family lineage.

If you have a family negative pattern of, say, addictions, poverty, divorce, greed, sickness, failure syndrome or selfishness, then you have a work to do. Don't be scared by the gravity or how long the problem has lasted. Don't say, "It has been there from the days of my ancestors and I can't do anything about it", rather, deal with it, by the power of God, you can put a stop to it. The good news is that we don't have to do the battle alone. God offers us the help of His Holy Spirit to equip and empower us to put a stop to the devils influences and enterprises in our family lineage.

Dealing with Bloodline Pattern is a Serious Business

Dealing with negative bloodline patterns is a serious business. It is more than breaking of curses. It follows a strategic process.

In a town in the North Central part of Nigeria, a man by name Ken got married to a lady called Tope. Before the marriage, Tope's family did everything possible to dissuade her from marrying the man. From history, people from the two villages do not intermarry.

The few people who have dared it either died early or separated after a period. However, Tope and Ken despised all warnings because they were deeply in love. They claimed that as Christians, they are not bound by unbiblical cultural beliefs. Unfortunately, they were not very devoted Christians.

Their prayer life was a big zero. They lacked what it takes to challenge the spiritual influences operational in their villages, and to make matters worse, they never consulted the word of God for direction.

After many battles with family members, they had their way. Their wedding ceremony was superlative. They were so glad that their dream of getting married materialized.

Their first two years of marriage was smooth. They had their first child without any issue. They thought in their hearts, "Where are the problems people predicted will happen to us if we marry? Our marriage has clocked two and nothing bad has happened". But troubles started in their third year of marriage. Tope got pregnant for the second child and had complications that caused severe bleeding during labour which necessitated a surgery. Unfortunately, she didn't come out of the theatre alive. She ended up the way many of her sisters who married in that village ended.

Another case is Martin and Luci from the same two villages who despised their people's warning and got married. Unlike Ken and Tope, they subjected themselves to serious prayers and they were extricated from the old evil pattern. Though the enemy tried severally to attack their family, they conquered through the blood.

The difference between these two families is that Ken's family did not understand spiritual principles. The fact that they have been called out of those kindred by the virtue of the new birth does not mean that the spirits in those kindred will not come for what legally binds the kindred's together.

Ken never understood the importance of undergoing deliverance prayers to severe his family from the old pattern that run in the two villages.

Martins understood the concept of spiritual warfare and the need to guard and defend his territory. He knew what it means to prevail in prayers and to make sacrifices through seed sowing. Consequently, against all predictions their marriage survived.

Once you discover a pattern in your family or community, you have to be willing to raise counter measures to silence the spirit from prevailing over you. This is done by constant and unswerving prayers, sowing seeds of faith and total surrender to Gods word.

Dealing with bloodline patterns requires deeper understanding of what you are actually dealing with. Someone may say, "Pastor, I was prayed for some time ago and every curse was broken in my family, but I still can't understand why the recurrence of the same issue.

What we are dealing with is more than just breaking of curses. It basically has to do with closing the door to the effects of sins or curses in the bloodline of a family. Even when a curse is broken in a family, or when a family repents of terrible sins committed in the past, what happens to the door that was opened to the devil by the family? Will your character change instantly because you got saved? No! It's not automatic. It takes a process.

You Have a Role to Play In Your Freedom

"And the Lord said unto Joshua,
see, I have given into thine hand Jericho,
and the king thereof, and the mighty men of valour."
(Josh. 6:2)

God appeared to Joshua and told him that he had given Jericho to them but there were still high walls that got them terribly frightened. Thank God for the Holy Spirit that told Joshua what to do to make his word come to pass (Joshua 6:3-5).

Think for a second, if Joshua did not adhere to the instructions of the Holy Ghost asking them to walk round the walls for seven times and blow the trumpet. I bet you, nothing would have happened. It wouldn't make God's word less powerful or less effective.

This is to let us know that even though God has a role to play in our victories over life challenges, we also must be involved in the process. We have the duties to denounce the evil of our father's house and also apply the word of God to enforce liberation. Hence, having the mindset that being a Christian makes all things fall into place, including all your needs, without playing your own role will predispose you to failure. You will never experience shouts of joy and victories in your camp with such warped attitude.

Steps in Dealing with Negative Bloodline Patterns

Step # 1
You Must Be Born Again

To be born again is the first step to overcoming negative bloodline pattern in your life. All the other steps we will discuss subsequently are secondary. They can only become efficacious if you understand the new life you received when you became a Christian.

To be born again means to be washed with the blood of Jesus. If you have not been washed by the blood of the Lamb, you are eminently qualified to be afflicted with the negative patterns that operate in your bloodline.

Being blood washed is important. According to the Law,

> "…almost all things are purified with blood, and without
> the shedding of blood there is no remission"
> **(Heb. 9:22).**

Generational curses are transmitted via the bloodline. So also, generational curses can be terminated and annulled by blood sacrifice. In the Old Testament, the blood of animals were used for cleansing and expiation, but in the new dispensation, the blood of Jesus suffices.

The blood of Jesus Christ that was shed on the cross of Calvary purchased for us total deliverance from all curses that we inherited and those we may have provoked by our evil actions. The moment we received the new life, every curse operational in our lives got broken from its foundation. The curses got broken at the instance of Christ death on the cross of Calvary. Scripture confirms this when it said:

> "He had redeemed us from the curse of the law, being made a curse for us: for it is written, "cursed is every one that hangeth on a tree..."
> **(Gal 3:13).**

Christ took our place and we in turn took his place. When he hung on the cross, he took our curses with him and gave us his blessings.

However, If any believer still experiences some traces of old pattern in his Life after he has confessed the Lordship of Jesus Christ, all he needs to do is to just get rid of it. He can do this by applying the principles below.

Step # 2
Discover and Acknowledge Negative Patterns

To deal effectively with negative patterns, you need to be wise and sensible enough to discern and conclude whether what is happening to you is normal with life's struggle or abnormal. There are challenges associated with life. These are normal. But when the challenges become so prevalent and persistent, or when you observe it in other members of your lineage, you should not push them aside with a wave of hand.

Discover the areas of your life where you constantly struggle. Note those bad lifestyles or habits you exhibit even though you know they are morally wrong. Don't trivialize patterns of divorce, wickedness, poverty, rise and fall syndrome or a pattern of sickness that occurs in the family. Don't say it is normal, or it is a coincidence. You can never change what you tolerate.

Step # 3
Confess and Denounce the Devil and His Properties

We have stated earlier that some spirits are responsible for many negative bloodline patterns in some families and societies. To kick the devil out and stop his evil enterprise, you must denounce him and reject his activities and properties. Every covenant made with the power of darkness has to be repudiated.

Two kings cannot rule the same kingdom. One has to be dethroned for the other to be enthroned. Until you dethrone the devil through the pronouncement of the withdrawal of your loyalty, God cannot come in.

Your words have power. All you need to do is to announce to the devil that your partnership with him is broken, then invite and ask God to take over. You will see how powerful God can be and how powerless the devil is.

Step #4
Dethrone the Strong Man Behind the Pattern

"Resist the devil and he will flee from you".
(Jam. 4:7 NIV)

The only language the devil understands is the language of fire. He doesn't honour words like:" Please. I am sorry. Have mercy…" So, to force him out and terminate his enterprises in your life, you must speak the language he will understand;

and that is the language of violence.

The bible has assured us that we can be extricated from our oppressors if we go into the battle with the Lord's backing. Isaiah the prophet says:

"Can plunder be taken from the warriors,
or captives rescued from the fierce? But this is what the Lord
says:
'Yes, captive will be taken from warriors And plunders retrieved
from the fierce;
I will contend with those who contend with you, and your
children I will save.
I will make your oppressors eat their own flesh;
they will be drunk on their own blood, as with wine.
Then all mankind will know that I, the Lord, am your saviour,
your redeemer,
the mighty one of Jacob'".
(Isa. 49:24 – 26 NIV)

Wow! What a promise; directly from the mouth of Yahweh Sabbaoth Himself. So you have no reason to fear the oppressor and his activities anymore.

Demand and insist that every familiar spirit that has been sent to your life, family or generation should lose its stronghold over you and your family. Tell the strong man to depart from your mind and give him reasons why he should leave as you speak. Terminate the appointment of the enemy working behind the scene, causing you havoc.

If you can't deal with this strong man, you can't possess your possession and claim your place.

The scripture confirms this in Mark 3:27:

"No man can enter into a strong man's house, and spoil his
goods, except he will first bind the strong man;
and then he will spoil his house".

Step #5
Speak Your Expectations into Your Life and Family

I have earlier stated that curses and negative bloodline patterns can be activated by negative pronouncements. After dethroning the strongman holding your family captive, the next thing should be to prophetically counter the negative pronouncements on your family by speaking positive things to your life and generation.

There is power in spoken words. So, speak to your bloodline. Declare what you want. Pass decrees with the power of the Holy Ghost in you. Reverse everything that is negative and pronounce blessings upon your life and family.

Since you are dealing with a bloodline pattern, be categorical in your pronouncements. Proclaim that the blessings you are announcing are for you and for generations to come. By so doing, you are clearing the way for generations unborn who would have laboured under the pattern if it was not terminated.

Step # 6
Raise an Altar

We have established earlier that one of the causes of bloodline negative patterns is Satanic altars–(physical or spiritual), raised by us or those before us in the lineage. One of the effective ways to deal with these altars, the powers behind them, and their evil enterprises is to raise a superior altar – God's altar. The battle now becomes altar versus altar. Of course we know that the superior altar, which is the altar of Yahweh, will always emerge supreme in any battle.

We raise an altar for Yahweh by dethroning the devil and enthroning Jesus as our king and master. The altar may not necessarily be physical as it was in the Old Testament. It symbolically means enthroning Jesus as our king – giving him a place in our family decisions and affairs.

Sustain Your Altar with Sacrifices

Altars are sustained by sacrifice. To keep your altar active, you need to be a man of sacrifice. If you want to see God do more things for you, think of what to do for Him. Inasmuch as your altar is alive and active; the doors to the devil and negative bloodline patterns will be permanently shut. "Give, it shall be giving unto you", is the key to tapping into God's blessings and prosperity. Giving is a special way of keeping your altar active.

Your seed will always speak for you at the gates of your enemies. It speaks for you before God.

There is nothing bad in studying great books on finance and wealth creation, but I tell you by revelation that if it is in your bloodline that you will never prosper by the reason of a transaction someone in your family made with the devil, you will be going round and round without success. You will be working like an elephant but eating like a grasshopper, because the devil has been given legal permission to hold your finances down for life. The solution therefore is not to apply human principles alone, but to apply godly principles also. Sowing of seeds to provoke your altar to speak for you is one of the godly principles you need to practice.

Most times, whenever a covenant is made between a man and the devil, there is always an exchange of substance with the devil before the covenant could be sealed. It could be a goat, a fowl, human blood, or any other substance. To terminate this covenant, most of us prefer to only pray and fast. Yes it works! But it is more complete when it is accompanied by sacrifice-giving.

Her Seed Terminated a Negative Pattern of Servitude

In chapter one of this book, I made mention of a lady I ministered to, who was a house-help in Lagos. To help her out of the bloodline pattern of servitude, I taught her the principles of sacrifice. I was led by the spirit to instruct her to sacrifice half of her salaries for the next three months to her church. She obeyed the voice of God.

Guess what happened! After the fifth month, through the connection of a friend, she partook in a contest, won and was offered a scholarship to study abroad. Within 3 years of living abroad, she helped her two siblings to travel abroad too.

The family that was nothing but slaves in the past became a family of reference in their town. All these blessings were provoked by the sacrifice of this lady.

His Seed Terminated Pattern of Untimely Death

A friend once shared a testimony of how his seed spoke for him and stopped the bloodline pattern of untimely death in his family. According to the testimony, one day, his elder brother had a dream where he was eating with some dead people. Two days after; he started having serious stomach pains and later died.

Few years after, his immediate elder brother had the same encounter in the dream, had stomach pains just like the elder brother and later died of the sickness in a hospital.

Guess what! Few years after; he had the same encounter like his two late brothers. He ate with some people in the dream; started having stomach pains like his late brothers did, and everyone was expecting him to die. To stop history from repeating itself, he rushed to the bank, withdrew an amount equivalent to his monthly salary and rushed to their church. He dropped the seed at the altar, prayed seriously and provoked the altar to rise against the evil altar at work in their family. Miraculously, my friend was delivered, and that pattern never repeated itself again in their family. Your seed will speak for you in the name of Jesus! Amen!

Step #7
Ask For Help If Need Be

Some personal problems are so entrenched that we need to be humble enough to ask for help. Don't be hesitant to call for help from a minister if you continue to struggle with a problem and realize you need additional support. There is no shame in asking for help and encouragement from others!

You must acknowledge that some people are more gifted than others in some areas of ministry. Seek help from such people if your personal efforts are not giving you the results you want. It is an act of pride to refuse to seek help when you need it.

Step #8
Work On Your Habits to Sustain Your Liberation

A habit is an acquired or learned behaviour we exhibit without even thinking about it. It is in us. It is part of us.

Most of our habits are developed from how we were raised in our families. If you were raised in a disorganized or lazy family, you will find out that waking up late will become a daily routine and going to work late will become normal.

While labouring under negative patterns, certain things became part of you. They became your lifestyle. Now that you have been delivered, you have to work on yourself.

Fight hard to get rid of old evil habits. Imbibe new habits that befit the saints in Zion.

Chapter 9

WALKING IN DIVINE BLESSING

"How blessed is the man who fears the Lord,
who greatly delights in His commandments.
His descendants will be mighty on earth;
the generation of the upright will be blessed."
(Psalm 112:1-2)

The bible pericope above is one of my best scriptures. I have read it several times, and each time I read it, I get deeper and newer revelation about our walk with God and the rewards that accompany it. This scripture speaks of mightiness and blessings for the upright and his descendants. It is one of the scriptures that open our eyes to the fact that in actuality, God's desire for His people is that they should be blessed.

After preaching this passage in one of our cell meetings, a young man asked me, "Pastor Chris, do you mean God really wants us to be blessed? You mean a child of God can become a super-star in different spheres of life? You mean we can occupy highly exalted positions in various sectors of life? Are you implying we can make news within our locality and internationally? You mean we can be sought after and used as reference point in some specific areas of life? You mean we can become trailblazers in our various areas of assignments? Wow! What a scripture!"

Yah! Without mincing words, that is God's Will for us. Though it may sound as tale by moonlight to many fanatical Christians who still live with unrefined mindset, but the truth cannot be changed.

God's plans for us are sure and well spelt out in the pages of the bible. Should the Holy Spirit open our eyes through the instrumentality of the scriptures, we will realize that many of us are living below the measure of blessings heaven has designed we should enjoy. The lives of many biblical heroes are testimonies to this allusion.

Jeremiah 29:11 says:

"I know the plans I have for you,
The plans to prosper you and give you a future full of hope."

The first time I read this scripture, I screamed on top of my voice. I was overwhelmed by the weight of the promises contained in this scripture. It seems so heavy for a natural man to contain because it baffles rationality.

Wow! Is this God's will for me? What a God! I never knew this all these years and I have been struggling. No wonder the bible says:

"My people perish for lack of knowledge" **(Hosea 4:6).**

My mind also leaped with inexplicable joy when I read Ephesians chapter 1 verse 3. It says:

"I have been blessed with all spiritual blessings in heavenly places".

After studying these and many other similar scriptures, my mindset changed. Quote me any day; there is nothing any man born of a woman, or any spirit from the pit of hell or even the angels can say, or do to change my belief that I am called to be blessed.

Blessings Can Be Transferred

It is remarkable to note that most blessings do not necessarily end with the man or woman who was blessed first or directly. If well managed, most times, the blessings trickle down to many generations following. It thus becomes what we term, "Generational blessings". Psalm112 verse 1-2 confirms this assertion.

God's ultimate desire is that we and the seeds that proceed from us should be blessed. Hence He told Abraham thus:

"In blessing I will bless thee, and in multiplying I will multiply
thy seed as the stars of the heaven
and as the sand which is upon the sea shore;
and thy seed shall possess the gate of his enemies"
(Gen.22:17)

Reading through the pages of the bible, we will notice that this blessings pronounced on Abraham impacted on the lives of Isaac and Jacob. Severally, in the bible, the Israelites laid claim to these blessings, and up to date, the Israelites have not ceased to appropriate the Abrahamic blessings pronounced centuries ago in the Old Testament.

Apart from the generational blessings exemplified in the bible, there is superfluity of examples of many other people outside the bible era who have enjoyed blessings in their bloodline. Most successful business men, renowned gospel ministers, academicians, politicians, etc. did not just emerge to limelight accidentally. Some of them are enjoying the seeds of greatness planted by someone in their lineage in the past.

In chapter four, I narrated the success account of Jonathan Edward, who lived in the 1700s, whose generation was tremendously blessed. I did state that he had eleven children, and according to history, he had this daily habit of laying hands and pronouncing blessings on them one after another. It worked. How do we know this?

In 1990, A.E Winship decided to trace and study the lineage of Jonathan Edwards. The result of his study was so amazing. It revealed that the lineage that started with
Jonathan Edward and his wife produced the following:

Three hundred preachers

Thirteen noted authors

Thirteen college presidents

Sixty five college professors

One hundred lawyers and a dean of a medical school

Thirty judges

Fifty six physicians and a dean of a medical school

Eighty holders of public office

Three United States senators

One vice president of the United States

One comptroller of the United States treasury

How to Attract Blessings

Recognize and Say No to Negative Bloodline Patterns

If all these sweet promises enumerated in many scriptures we have studied above are actually for us believers, why then do we keep quiet and tolerate negative bloodline patterns as if they are normal? Why do we allow the enemy to mesmerize our precious lives with the ugly and detestable things happening in various families? The point is that we are called to be blessed and to be a blessing and not be influenced by the evil of our father's house.

So we must recognize when things are going wrong in our family lineage and be bold enough to denounce and confront them. Most importantly, we must dispose ourselves to receive the blessings that are appropriate for true believers.

Desire to Be Blessed

As a believer, don't just be relaxed that you are born again; you also need to move ahead. Remember, it was your spirit that received a new life when you got born again and not your body; it is now your responsibility to create a new blessed pattern for yourself and your family. So, think of the big picture, make plans to leave your family line better than you met it. Make things easier for the next generation.

Remember, every lap you run is one less lap for the next person to come.

Provoke Your Generational Blessing

Just as curses can be provoked and activated in a man's life or in a lineage, blessings can also be activated in a man's life or in a lineage. In other words, nothing just happens. Every action will always have a reaction.

Most times, blessings can come as an unmerited favour. That is to say that in most cases, you are blessed not really because you worked for it, but because it pleased the one blessing you to favour you. This is called "Unmerited blessings". But there is another kind of blessings and greatness that come to a man and his generation consequent upon his good works. These blessings come as a reward for his works. This is the kind of blessing Psalm 112:1-2, is talking about.

It is so encouraging that the little efforts we make to be good are not in vain. There is a reward for every good deed.

Blessings can be in the form of tangible things such as: children, money, cars, landed properties and many others. It can also be in the form of intangible things, such as, long life, wisdom, sound intellect, talents, good health, amongst others.

Always Play By the Rules

When a man lives according to God's dictates, it provokes blessings. Therefore, always make it a duty to do right always. Be a blessing to others, you and your children will surely reap the fruits. Live under divine rules in order to avoid calamity.

Stay far from idolatry, greed, pride and anger. Embrace love, joy, and a giving heart. By so doing, your bloodline will inherit a lineage filled with pleasant patterns.

Provoke Blessings with Your Seeds

To the best of your ability, help other people who are in need of your assistance. It is a sure way of attracting divine blessings. There is always a reward for every good deed done to people, communities and nations. No works go unrewarded.

America is a typical example of a nation that understands how to provoke divine blessing for the now and future generation. They do so by helping other countries in need. Endeavour to help others and your generation will never lack help.

PRAYER NUGGETS

- Any door that anyone in my family opened, that gave the enemy the legal right to torture or harass me, let it be interrupted, let it backfire in the name of Jesus!

- I address every yoke of poverty, limitation, hindrance, restriction, servitude over my life in the name of Jesus.

- Any demonic pregnancy and conception in the womb of the enemy that has been programmed in the womb of time to determine my circumstances, to influence events in my life, let that pregnancy and conception be interrupted and terminated in the name of Jesus. I overturn it, I interrupt, intercept and override it in the name of Jesus.

- I break the stronghold of the enemy against my life and that of my family.

In the name of Jesus, I BREAK OUT, I BREAK LOOSE, I BREAK FREE, I BREAK FORTH.

- I revoke the curses of my bloodline.

- I release myself from my father's demon.

- I release myself from my mother's demon.

- I release myself from the demons of my bloodline.

- I bind the strong man of my bloodline and of my DNA in the name of Jesus.

- Satan! Take your hands off me. Take your hands off my body, Take your hands off my health. Take your hands off my marriage. Take your hands off my family in the name of Jesus Christ.

- I interrupt every contention over my life, over my destiny, over my health, over my finances and over my seed in the name of Jesus!

- I command it now to backfire in the name of Jesus It shall not stand neither shall it come to pass

- I interrupt Satan's plan for my life.

- Every plan of the enemy for my life. I terminate! I terminate!! I terminate!!!

- I bind the strong man of my family.

- Let the curses over my life be broken! Let the curses over my family be broken! (Put your hands together and command it to break).

- I block every access by which the enemy uses to attack me in my dreams.

- I cancel every evil dream.

- I bind every familiar spirit.

- I rebuke the power of death, of the grave and of hell over me in the name of Jesus.

- And I hereby put on strength. For it is God that girdeth me with strength to the battle.

- I am free and my soul has escaped as the bird out of the snare of the fowler in the name of Jesus!

AMEN!!!

Other Books by Chris Emeruo

- **"Roadmap to Eternal Life"** is a free mini book by Chris Emeruo distributed across the country free of charge for Evangelism.

For free copies of the Roadmap to Eternal Life for evangelism, contact:

RIVERSIDE PUBLICATION P.O Box 13159 IKEJA, LAGOS.

- **Living Positive In Negative Environment**

We all are surrounded by hostile people - unfriendly staff, envious business associates, uncaring family members, economically harsh nation, amongst others. Our dreams are suppressed each day by other people.

Day by day, we encounter people who talk us down and hinder us from moving to the next level of life.

This masterpiece teaches how to maintain our cool in the heat of worldly pressures.

Available in Bookstores Nationwide.

Connect with Chris Emeruo

Website: www.chrisemeruo.org
Email: info@chrisemeruo.org
Facebook: www.facebook.com/Chrisemeruo
Twitter: www.Twitter.com/Chrisemeruo
Instagram: www.Instagram.com/Chrisemeruo